BERG, ANNEMARIE
Great Seals of the U.S.

Great State Seals
of the
United States

Great State Seals
of the
United States

ANNEMARIE BERG

Dodd, Mead & Company • New York

ACKNOWLEDGMENTS

Many thanks are due for the cooperation of all the state officials—
governors, lieutenant governors, secretaries of state, and their
assistants.
A special debt of gratitude goes to those custodians of history, the
state archivists, librarians, and historical societies of every state who
provided the history of each seal.
Without their generous cooperation this book could not have been
written.

ILLUSTRATION CREDITS: Minnesota Historical Society, page 78; South
Dakota State Historical Society, page 131.

2   3   4   5   6   7   8   9   10

Library of Congress Cataloging in Publication Data

Berg, Annemarie.
Great State seals of the United States.

SUMMARY: Discusses the design, adoption, and use of
the Great Seals of the 50 states.
1.   Seals (Numismatics)—United States—Juvenile
literature. [1.   Seals (Numismatics)]   I.   Title.
CD5603.B47   737'.6'0973   79-52035
ISBN 0-396-07705-6

TO ALL REFERENCE LIBRARIANS—
THE STUDENTS' BEST FRIEND

California's Secretary of State, March Fong Eu, impressing the State Seal on an official document. This elaborate hand-operated seal press, bought in 1873, stands four feet high and holds a die engraved in 1891.

What Is a Seal?

A seal is a design or device engraved on a metal disc which stamps an impression in wax or paper. Today the design is intended to represent a governing body, institution, company, corporation, or individual and is used to validate legal documents. Originally seals, which date back to ancient times, were used in place of written signatures as few people could read or write in those days.

The Great Seal of a state represents the highest authority of that state, and a governor cannot govern without the use of a state seal. It is the signature of the state and must appear on all important documents, proclamations, patents, commissions, and state papers to make them official.

Either the governor, lieutenant governor, or the secretary of state has charge of the Great Seal. This involves a moral obligation which officials take very seriously. In fact, Georgia's secretary of state and keeper of the seal was prepared to die to protect it from Sherman's army during the Civil War.

During the Middle Ages use of seals by the church and nobility flourished, but by the thirteenth century, merchants, craftsmen, guilds, and town officials were also using seals. Many of these depicted tools of a trade or symbols of an office as means of identification. Most state seals follow this custom by featuring some part of their history, politics, or resources, making the seal uniquely theirs. Much can be learned about a state simply by studying its seal.

An official seal is important to running a government. So much so that the First Continental Congress appointed a committee to select a fitting seal for the new nation only a few hours after declaring Independence on July 4, 1776. John Adams, Benjamin Franklin, and Thomas Jefferson headed the committee that eventually selected a symbol that best represented the values and beliefs of our Founding Fathers. This symbol, the Great Seal of the United States, appears on all one dollar bills.

In early days, seals were hand-engraved and embedded in a seal press. A warmed wax wafer placed on the document was then inserted in the press under the seal. By pushing down a handle, the engraved seal stamped an impression in the warm wax and adhered it firmly to the official paper. However, the use of wax has long been discontinued.

Today seals are automatically engraved on a brass disc or die by a reduction machine. A counterseal is cast from the brass die and both are put into the press so the upper one fits snugly into the lower counterseal. A document is slipped between the two dies and compressed either by hand or automatically. This forces the two dies into each other, leaving a deep and clear impression in the paper. Usually a gold or colored paper disc, glued to the left-hand corner of the paper, receives the official impression. Though the engraved die in the seal press is actually the seal, the impressions it makes are also called seals.

Anyone desiring a picture or reproduction of their state seal may write to the secretary of state.

✳══════ Alabama ══════✳

When Alabama became a territory in 1817, President James Monroe appointed William W. Bibbs first territorial governor. A congressional law permitted the governor to choose his own seal, so Governor Bibbs ordered one showing the map of the territory featuring its great rivers. As there were no good roads in those days, all commerce and heavy shipping went by river. Bibbs felt that the rivers, being a most important resource of the state, should be honored on the seal. Around this seal were the words ALABAMA EXECUTIVE OFFICE, and only the governor used the seal.

Two years later, in 1819, Alabama became the twenty-second state. The wording on the seal was changed to ALABAMA GREAT SEAL, and the secretary of state became custodian. This seal remained in use for fifty years.

After the Civil War, in 1868, during the Reconstruction Period, carpetbaggers took over state politics and abolished the

old seal. The Reconstruction legislation adopted a new seal consisting of an eagle on a shield. In its beak the eagle held a scroll with the words "Here We Rest." This inscription came from an Indian legend by an Alabama writer in which the Indian word *Alabama* meant "Here We Rest." However, years later, the writer admitted he had made up the Indian legend, and it was actually fiction. Other men who had studied the meaning of the word said Alabama meant "This is a goodly land, and here we will make our home." For the next seventy years the Reconstruction seal remained the Great State Seal, though there was still resentment among native Alabamans over the loss of their original seal.

In 1939, the legislature passed on a bill sponsored by the Alabama United Daughters of the Confederacy to restore the old seal as the Great Seal of Alabama. When the bill came up for action there was not a dissenting vote in either the House or the Senate. The secretary of state immediately ordered a new seal engraved. Once more the seal bears the map of Alabama and its magnificent rivers just as Governor Bibbs had designed it.

The secretary of state is custodian of the Great Seal of Alabama.

13

 Alaska

Russia sold Alaska to the United States in 1867, and it was known as the District of Alaska until 1912. Then Washington, D.C., designated it as an organized territory until 1959, when Alaska became the forty-ninth state.

When still a district, the first governor, on his own motion and without instructions from Washington, designed a seal and had it made. This design featured icebergs, northern lights, a native fishing through the ice, and igloos. For the next twenty-five years it remained the seal of the district.

In 1910, District Governor Walter E. Clark felt the seal placed too much emphasis on natives, northern lights, and icebergs. He commissioned an "unnamed draughtsman" to design a sketch according to his specifications that would represent the industries of Alaska. The governor sent the sketch to the Secretary of the Interior in Washington, D.C. Someone in the department made a more refined sketch which was approved, and Governor Clark

received the new official seal which he turned over to the district secretary. That design is the same one used today.

The rays above the mountains are the northern lights, or aurora borealis, for which Alaska is famous. The smelter at the left represents mining, and the train with flatcars stands for transportation by rail, while ships in the bay represent transportation by sea.

Trees indicate the lumber industry and forests of the state; a farmer and his horses, with three shocks of wheat in the field, symbolize agriculture. In the outer circle, the fish at the right and the mother seal and baby on the left signify the importance of fishing and seal rookeries to Alaska's economy.

This first official seal was surrounded by the words THE SEAL OF THE DISTRICT OF ALASKA. Later the word DISTRICT was changed to TERRITORY. Upon attaining statehood, the wording was changed to THE SEAL OF THE STATE OF ALASKA.

The lieutenant governor of Alaska is custodian of the Great State Seal.

✳══════Arizona══════✳

The only feature of this seal that has survived from the original territorial seal is the motto *Ditat Deus*, meaning "God Enriches."

Arizona did not become the forty-eighth state until 1912, but the constitutional convention anticipated statehood within the next year or so, and adopted a state seal designed in 1910. A Phoenix newspaper artist E. M. Motter prepared a sketch showing the great industries and resources of the state.

The sun rising over the mountains indicates the fair climate and sunshine; a storage reservoir of water held back by a dam provides water for irrigated fields and orchards below. Agriculture is one of the state's main industries. A miner with pick and shovel and the quartz mill on the hillside represent mining, especially copper for which Arizona is noted. A cow grazing in the foreground symbolizes the huge cattle business of the state. Surrounding these are the words GREAT SEAL OF THE STATE OF ARIZONA and the year 1912, date of statehood. However, this seal

was adopted only after a bitter dispute at the Constitutional Convention of 1910. Those in favor of the new design were vigorously opposed by a contingent of delegates who held out for the Territorial Seal of 1864.

Originally, Richard C. McCormick, first secretary of the territory, brought a seal from the East with him in 1863. His seal bore the motto *Ditat Deus* and featured a miner standing cross-legged, with a pick and shovel, against a background of two mountains. However, this design resembled the trademark on a popular brand of baking powder, and soon it became known as the "baking powder" seal.

Maybe it was the stigma of "baking powder," but the first territorial assembly, meeting in 1864, adopted a new seal. The cross-legged miner was replaced by a deer, pine trees, and "columnar cactus" (the saguaro).

It was this cactus seal the old-timers wanted to keep. The 1910 committee chairman for a new seal explained that they "wanted to get away from cactus, Gila monsters and rattle snakes and feature Arizona's great storage dams, irrigated fields, cattle and mines."

To which an opposing delegate replied, "I would like to see that old cactus back in the seal. The work of nature is better than the work of man . . . that dam may not be here 50 years from now but the cactus will not be gone from Arizona."

The next day the seal vote came up and the old-timers lost, 11 to 28. But all members agreed to keep the motto *Ditat Deus*.

The secretary of state is custodian of the Great Seal of Arizona.

Arkansas

When Arkansaw (later changed to Arkansas) became a territory in 1819, Judge Samuel Calhoun Roane was asked to design the territorial seal which was adopted in 1820.

He was well qualified for this, being an expert in heraldry, symbols, and emblems. For the new design he borrowed heavily from other seals, taking the arrows, olive branch, and thirteen stars (representing the thirteen original states) from the Great Seal of the United States. From Pennsylvania's seal, he took the shield; from North Carolina, the Goddess of Liberty, with her liberty cap and pole. Then he embellished the design with an Angel of Mercy, the Sword of Justice, and two eagles. To show the industries of Arkansas he included a steamboat for transportation, a plow and beehive for industry, and a shock of wheat to represent agriculture. The motto on this design was *Regnant Populi*, meaning "Let the People Rule."

When Arkansas became the twenty-fifth state on June 15,

1836, the territorial seal with the word STATE substituted for TERRITORY became the official seal. In 1864 the two eagles were eliminated and a single one replaced them in the center of the design. The last change in the seal came in 1907 when the motto was altered to *Regnat Populus*, which means "The People Rule." This is the state motto.

In most states the secretary of state is custodian of the seal. However, Arkansas is one of the exceptions. The governor is keeper of the seal and state documents are "issued in the name and by the authority of the State of Arkansas, sealed by the Great Seal of the State, signed by the Governor and attested by the Secretary of State." Each state and county official uses a seal designed exactly like the Great State Seal, except the wording indicates their office. Therefore, the secretary of state's seal reads: GREAT SEAL OF THE SECRETARY OF STATE, ARKANSAS.

✳══════ California ══════✳

When California became the thirty-first state in 1850, the Constitutional Convention of 1849 had already provided for a state seal and adopted a design submitted by Major R. S. Garnett. There was only one complaint from someone who wanted "bags of gold and bales of merchandise" instead of the bear. While there have been a few changes in Garnett's design over the years, basically the seal today is that of 1849.

Thirty-one stars around the top signify that California was the thirty-first state in the Union. Below is the state motto *Eureka*, meaning "I have found it!" Mountain peaks of the Sierra Nevada stand for the grandeur of nature, while the sailing ships typify commerce. The Goddess Minerva, sprung full-blown from the brain of Jupiter, typifies the political birth of California without having gone through the probation of territory. Minerva is also Goddess of the Arts and Sciences, wise in peace and war. At her feet is a grizzly bear, symbol of the state of California.

Agricultural wealth is indicated by the sheaf of wheat. The miner working with pick and shovel, rocker and pan, represents industry and the golden wealth of the state. Surrounding the design are the words THE GREAT SEAL OF THE STATE OF CALIFORNIA.

That first convention of 1849 directed that "the seal, press and all appendages" should be delivered to the secretary of state.

Instead, they were delivered to the governor, who kept them until 1850 when he turned them over to the secretary "as a matter of convenience."

Five years later, in 1855, the seal became the center of a conflict between Governor John Bigler and Secretary of State J. W. Denver. The secretary ran for the United States Congress and won the election. He left for Washington, D.C., on October 4, leaving his resignation effective on November 5. The governor felt that the state was without a secretary and asked for Denver's immediate resignation. If refused, the governor would declare the office vacant and appoint a new secretary. Possibly Governor Bigler recalled that the first governor had charge of the seal for a while, and he asked that the state seal "be hereinafter kept in the governor's office." However, Denver defiantly refused to either resign or give the seal to the newly appointed secretary, saying the "office is not vacant." This stalemate continued until November 5 and not until then did the governor and the new secretary obtain the seal.

In 1945, a statute made the secretary of state official keeper of the Great State Seal of California.

✳ ══ Colorado ══ ✳

When Colorado became a territory in 1861, Lewis L. Weld, the young territorial secretary who had been appointed by President Lincoln, designed the official seal. He may have had some help from the first territorial governor, William Gilpin, as both men were experts in heraldry and symbolism.

Since mining was of primary importance in those early days, Mr. Weld placed the miner's badge of crossed pickax and hammer against a golden background in the lower part of a shield; the upper part, with three snowcapped mountain peaks and clouds against a red background, represents the beautiful mountains of Colorado. Above the shield a bundle of sticks bound around an ax symbolizes the strength lacking in only a single stick, while the ax stands for authority and leadership. This is called a fasces and comes from an old Roman custom of carrying a bundle of rods fastened around an ax in front of a magistrate as an emblem of his official power. This can also be interpreted as the insignia

26

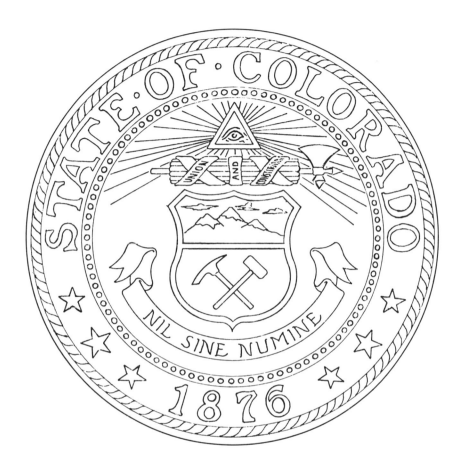

of a republican form of government. The banding on the fasces, with the words "Union and Constitution," is red, white, and blue.

The Eye of God, also part of the United States Great Seal, casts golden rays over the fasces and shield. The state motto, *Nil Sine Numine*, means "Nothing Without the Deity." However, irreverent miners of those days interpreted *Nil Sine Numine* as "Nothing Without a New Mine."

In 1876, a hundred years after the Declaration of Independence, Colorado became the thirty-eighth state. The first general assembly provided for an official state seal, but being frugal men, they did not have a new seal cast. Instead they had the territorial seal altered to read STATE instead of TERRITORY and substituted the statehood date of 1876 for 1861. For sixty-six dollars a local engraving company did this work and also made the Supreme Court seal.

State statutes had only partly described the colors of the seal and when reproduced the colors were never alike. To celebrate Colorado's Centennial year of statehood in 1976, the secretary of state announced a coloring contest open to school children in the third, fourth, fifth, and sixth grades to decide the "official color design for the Great Seal of Colorado."

On May 19, 1976, Stephanie Samaras, a fourth grader, was declared the official winner. Her colors were "to be used whenever the Great Seal of Colorado is prepared in color." This makes Colorado the only state in which a junior citizen took part in their state's Great Seal.

* ═══ Connecticut ═══ *

Connecticut, fifth of the original thirteen states, ratified the Constitution in 1788. During the years it was a colony there were several colonial seals but all had the same theme as today's state seal.

One of the earliest of these seals depicted a vineyard with fifteen vines and a hand reaching down from a cloud with the motto that is in use today. This elaborate seal was replaced with a simpler one that had only three vines. Surrounding the design was the Latin inscription SIGILLUM COLONIAE CONNECTICUTENSIS, meaning "Seal of the Colony of Connecticut."

In 1784 the general assembly decided this seal was inappropriate as Connecticut was no longer a colony. The assembly ordered a new seal which was to be inscribed SIGILL. REIP. CONNECTICUTENSIS. However, the inscription was engraved without the abbreviations and the assembly approved it the way it came from the engraver. Possibly they had changed their minds about the abbreviations.

This official seal "to be lodged with the Secretary to be used as the seal of this State" was engraved on a silver plate and soldered to a brass base. When this silver die wore out from use it was presented to Yale University and a new die cast in brass.

The double ring around the seal contains the Latin words SIGILLUM REIPUBLICAE CONNECTICUTENSIS, meaning "The Seal of the Republic of Connecticut." Three flourishing vines, each bearing four leaves and three bunches of grapes, symbolize the colony which came over here from England and established itself in the wilderness of America. On the ribbon below the vines is the state motto, *Qui Transtulit Sustinet*, which translated from the Latin means, "He who transplanted, sustains." This theme comes from Psalm 80: "Thou hast brought a vine out of Egypt; Thou hast cast out the heathen and planted it." The motto can also be interpreted to mean, "He who brought over the vine continues to take care of it."

The secretary of state is custodian of the Great State Seal of Connecticut.

 Delaware

Delaware was the first of the original thirteen states to ratify the Federal Constitution and consequently is nicknamed "The First State."

When the general assembly met in 1776, a committee was appointed to select a seal for the new state. They chose a simple design consisting of a figure of Britannia pointing to a figure of Liberty with the words "Go To America." However, an expert in heraldry told the committee this design was more suited to a medal than a state seal, so the committee went back to selecting a new and more appropriate design. Meantime, as the government could not operate without an official seal, the seal of New Castle County was to be used until there was a state seal.

Unfortunately, the British invaded New Castle County, seized the state records, and took the temporary seal away with them. The legislature immediately ordered the seal of Kent County to be used pending a new state seal.

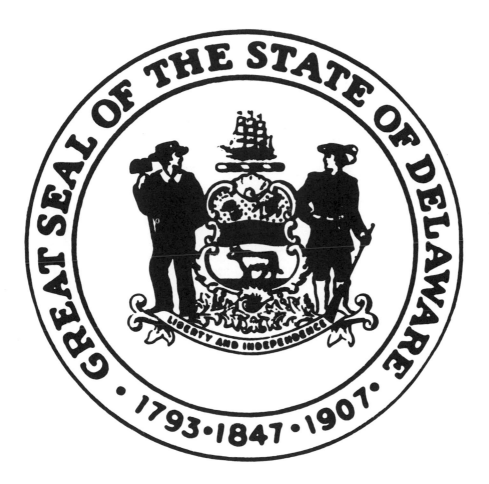

The following year, in January, 1777, the legislature adopted the design submitted by the committee for a seal, which was then engraved on a silver disc. This design, with slight modifications over the years, is the seal of today.

A sheaf of wheat and an ear of Indian corn in the upper part of the shield, with an ox standing below them, symbolize agriculture which is an important industry in Delaware. A band dividing the ox from the wheat and corn represents a river, and the sailing ship above the shield stands for commerce. At the left of the shield a farmer also symbolizes agriculture, while the soldier on the right indicates that Delaware fought in the battle for Independence. Not until 1847 was the state motto, "Liberty and Independence," added.

Around the design is the inscription GREAT SEAL OF THE STATE OF DELAWARE. The three dates—1793, 1847, 1907—are the years in which slight changes were made in the seal.

The secretary of state is custodian of the Great Seal of Delaware.

Florida

Florida became the twenty-seventh state in 1845 but continued to use its territorial seal for another year.

Seven years earlier, the territory, anticipating statehood, called a general assembly in 1838 to draw up a constitution for the future state. At the same time they provided for an official seal; "The first elected Governor should select the new seal design. Until such time as the Governor presented a seal, the territorial seal would remain the seal of the State." William D. Moseley, first elected governor, exercised this constitutional right and the assembly adopted his design in 1846. It was an elaborate seal featuring a map of Florida, four ships, an island, four trees, and an Indian female.

Succeeding governors and officials did not like the seal and in 1868 adopted the design that, with several modifications, is the seal of today. Historians agree that the artist who designed this 1868 seal had never been to Florida. About the size of a silver

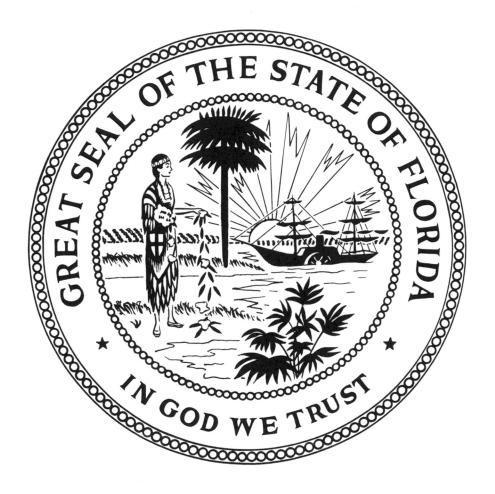

dollar, it had the sun rising over a mountain in the distance, a cocoa tree, a steamboat on water, and an Indian female scattering flowers in the foreground. Circling the design were the words GREAT SEAL OF THE STATE OF FLORIDA. Below was the state motto, "In God We Trust."

As Florida has no mountains for the sun to rise over, it was obvious the artist did not know the state or the Indians of that area. The Indian woman in his seal wore the feathered headdress of Northern tribes worn only by chiefs or warriors. As one man wrote, "When the 1868 artist put the crown of eagle feathers on his Indian female he presented Florida with an unclassified savage having the head of a warrior and the body of a squaw."

This design has been corrected and modified to the present seal. The nonexistent mountains were removed and the sun, for which Florida is famous, shines unhindered. The side-wheeler boat represents transportation. Symbolic of the first inhabitants of this country, the Indian female, minus the feathered headdress, looks exactly as an Indian girl should. The cocoa tree has been defined by the 1970 legislature as a sabal palmetto palm, which is the official state tree.

The secretary of state is custodian of the Great State Seal of Florida.

═══ Georgia ═══

The fourth state of the original thirteen to ratify the Federal Constitution, Georgia adopted a state seal at the first convention in 1777. This design is said to be the work of Button Gwinnett, one of the signers of the Declaration of Independence. It consisted of a scroll bearing the words "The Constitution of the State of Georgia" and a motto *Pro Bono Publico*, meaning "For the Public Good." However, the first state constitution conflicted in places with the United States Constitution, so another convention met in 1799 to adopt a new state constitution and a new seal, which is the state seal in use today.

Three pillars supporting the arch "Constitution" represent the three branches of government—legislative, judicial, and executive. The words around the pillars are also the state motto, "Wisdom, Justice, Moderation," and apply to each government branch. The soldier with drawn sword represents Georgia's military aid in defense of the Constitution. Originally 1799 appeared on this

seal, but the 1914 legislature officially changed it to 1776, date of the Declaration of Independence and birth of the state.

During the Civil War, Secretary of State Colonel N. C. Barnett saved the seal from falling into the hands of the enemy. Fearing the Yankees might kill him, he took the seal home and gave it to his wife to hide so someone else would know the location of the seal. She buried it under the house in a tin box. When Sherman reached the capital, which was then Milledgeville, he arrested Barnett and demanded the state seal. Barnett refused, saying he would die first. Though Sherman imprisoned the secretary, they never found the seal. At the end of the war Barnett dug up the seal.

The state seal was in jeopardy again when Georgia was placed under military rule in 1868. Republicans, radicals, and carpetbaggers swarmed into the state to take over the government. A convention of carpetbaggers demanded forty thousand dollars for expense money from the state treasurer. He refused, saying the law prohibited payment except on order of the governor. Governor Charles J. Jenkins refused to honor their demand and was forced out of office. He promptly withdrew $400,000 from the state treasury, took the state seal, and fled to New York. He put the money and seal in a vault for safekeeping, where they remained for four years. In 1872 when Georgia's own people regained possession of the state government, Jenkins returned the seal and money, which he had "held as a sacred trust for his people." For this patriotic act Jenkins received a Resolution of Gratitude from the state and a gold facsimile of the seal. These are now in possession of the Georgia Historical Society in Savannah.

The secretary of state is custodian of the Great State Seal of Georgia.

 Hawaii

This is the only state that was a kingdom, a republic, and a territory before taking its place as the fiftieth and last state in the Union.

When Hawaii became a republic in 1894, a local artist named Viggo Jacobsen designed the seal, basing part of it on the coat-of-arms of the kingdom. The Republican Legislature of 1896 adopted his design for the official seal. This first seal bore the words REPUBLIC OF HAWAII and 1894 in Roman numerals. Upon becoming a territory the wording was changed to TERRITORY OF HAWAII, with the date 1900. Since joining the Union the seal reads STATE OF HAWAII and 1959, date of statehood. This is still the same design created by Jacobsen.

King Kamehameha I (unifier of the Hawaiian kingdom) stands on one side of the center shield. On the other side is the Goddess of Liberty holding the Hawaiian flag. On the first and fourth quarters of the shield are the eight stripes of the Ha-

waiian flag, which also represent the eight major islands. In the
other two quarters, the ball on a staff represents *puloulou* or tabu
sticks. These were carried before chiefs in ancient Hawaii or
placed in front of the doors of their houses. They denoted power
and authority. The star in the center of the shield formerly stood
for the star that would be added to the American flag when

Hawaii became a state. Now it represents the fiftieth star in the flag.

The rising sun symbolized the birth of the new republic, but now symbolizes the birth of the state. The phoenix signifies a democratic government rising from the ashes of a monarchy. Surrounding them are taro and banana leaves with sprays of maidenhair fern, all typical of the state. Around the bottom of the seal is the motto *Ua·mau·ke·ea·o·ka·aina·i·ka·pono*, meaning "The Life of the Land Is Perpetuated in Righteousness." King Kamehameha III gave this motto to the kingdom in 1843, and it has been the motto of the republic, territory, and now the state.

The lieutenant governor of Hawaii is custodian of the Great State Seal.

Idaho

Probably one of the most beautiful and impressive of all seals is that of Idaho. It is also the only state seal designed by a woman.

In 1890, the year Idaho became our forty-third state, Emma Sarah Edwards, a young art student who had been studying in New York, visited Boise. She fell in love with the bustling frontier town with its beautiful scenery and opened a studio to teach painting.

Idaho already had a territorial seal, but with statehood the first legislature naturally wanted a state seal. Famous artists from all over the country were invited to enter a competition for a new seal design, and a special committee would select the best one. The young art teacher, Emma Edwards, submitted a painting which won by unanimous vote of the committee. On March 5, 1891, Governor Norman B. Willey presented her with the first prize of one hundred dollars.

Emma's design shows a woman with scales and liberty cap to

represent Justice and Liberty; the man typifies Idaho's great mineral and gem mining industry. Farming is represented by the shock of wheat, and the cornucopias spilling a plentiful harvest of fruit and vegetables. A close look shows potatoes in the cornucopia of vegetables. This must have been foresight on the part of Miss Edwards as Idaho is now famous for potatoes, and it is highly

45

appropriate that they should be on the state seal. Pictured on the shield in the center of the seal are the scenic mountains of Idaho as a background for the plowman and horse which represent agriculture. The tall tree at the right symbolizes the timber and lumber industry. The state motto, *Esto Perpetua*, which means "Exist Forever," also appears on the state flag.

Many years later, in 1957, the two figures on the original design were modernized and updated. Engraving and casting the new seal cost one thousand dollars, ten times the prize money Emma received. This slight alteration did not change the original concept of the seal. Miss Edwards' prizewinning painting is held in trust by the Idaho Historical Society in Boise.

The secretary of state is custodian of the Great State Seal of Idaho.

 Illinois

When Illinois became a territory in 1809, an almost exact copy of the Great Seal of the United States without the motto *E Pluribus Unum* served as their official seal. Today's seal, though greatly changed, is based on that first design.

In 1818 Illinois became the twenty-first state, and the following year the first general assembly decreed that "it was the duty of the Secretary of State to procure a permanent state seal." His choice would have to be agreeable to the governor and the Supreme Court justices.

This 1818 seal also was a duplicate of the national seal, but this time the eagle held in its beak a scroll on which was the motto "State Sovereignty—National Union." In one talon the eagle held the arrows of war or strength, in the other the olive branch of peace, and on its breast was a shield. This seal remained in use until 1868.

Secretary of State Sharon Tyndale told a senator in 1867 that

47

Illinois

the old seal was worn out, he needed a new one, and asked the senator to sponsor a bill to renew it. The bill passed the Senate without question and went to the House. One of the members suggested an amendment to provide that the new seal was to be "an exact facsimile of the present seal." While this amendment

48

was defeated, it raised a question about the new seal and the bill went back to the Senate for further discussion. It was discovered that Tyndale planned to reverse the wording of the motto to read "National Union—State Sovereignty." No one knows why he wanted to make this change, but a Senate amendment ruled that the words of the state motto were to remain the same as on the old seal.

A new seal engraved in 1868 is the same one in use today and was also designed by Secretary Tyndale. It differed considerably from the old one. The eagle now perches on a boulder in a prairie. Two dates appear on the boulder—1868 when the seal was adopted, and 1818 date of statehood. The shield, formerly on the eagle's breast, is tilted on the ground. The arrows were eliminated and only the olive branch remains. The motto was unchanged and around the design is inscribed SEAL OF THE STATE OF ILLINOIS and the statehood date, Aug. 26th, 1818.

The secretary of state is custodian of the Great State Seal of Illinois.

Indiana

This state seal is unusual because it was not legal until 1963, 147 years after Indiana became the nineteenth state in 1816.

For a seal to be official, the state constitution first authorizes a seal. A design is then submitted for approval to the legislature, which then votes on it. If they adopt the design it is so written into the state records, along with a complete description of the seal.

In the case of Indiana, the first general assembly of 1816 did provide for a seal, and there was a brief description of it. But the assembly did not vote on it. Again, in 1859, the matter of a legal seal came before the assembly. A committee reported on it at great length, but once more the bill was not voted upon by the time the session adjourned.

Indiana did not operate without a seal, legal or not. The state used variations of the territorial seal which the first territorial

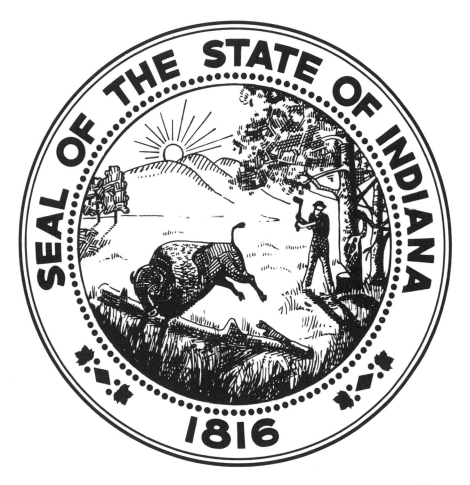

governor, William Henry Harrison, had brought with him from Philadelphia.

An alert researcher with the legislative bureau discovered that Indiana's seal was not legal and brought this to the attention of state officials and newspapers. In 1963 the general assembly and the governor approved the seal which was then described in great detail for the records and voted upon. The seal they adopted is almost exactly like the one Governor Harrison used for the territory.

The full sun setting over the mountain probably indicated the setting of old ways as civilization moved in. Some historians think the buffalo did not belong on the seal as Indiana was never their home. But these animals did graze in the state and so the buffalo was acceptable on the seal. The pioneer woodsman signified the clearing of land as agriculture moved in. Surrounding this historical scene are the words SEAL OF THE STATE OF INDIANA and 1816, date of statehood. On either side of the date is a design consisting of a diamond with four dots and two leaves of the tulip tree, Indiana's official state tree.

According to the state constitution, the governor has custody of the Great State Seal of Indiana.

Iowa

Territorial Secretary William B. Conway designed the territorial seal adopted in 1838. The sketch consisted of an eagle, "the proud and appropriate emblem of our national power," holding an arrow in its beak and an unstrung bow in one talon. Surrounding the eagle were the words SEAL OF THE TERRITORY OF IOWA. Secretary Conway took his design to a William Wagner of York, Pennsylvania, to be engraved, and a die of this original territorial seal has been preserved by the State Historical Society.

Iowa became the twenty-ninth state in 1846, but nineteen days before actual statehood a bill authorized the secretary to procure a new seal, and forty dollars was appropriated for it.

The new seal bore the words THE GREAT SEAL OF THE STATE OF IOWA, surrounding a sheaf of wheat and field of standing wheat with sickle and other farming utensils symbolizing agriculture; a lead furnace and pile of ingots representing the lead mining at Dubuque; a citizen soldier carrying the American flag and liberty

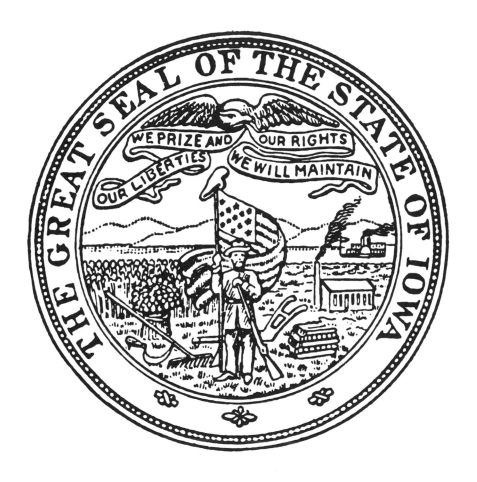

cap in his right hand, a gun in his left, indicating patriotism and preparedness to fight for the Union. At the rear is the Mississippi River with the steamboat *Iowa* representing transportation. At the upper edge an eagle, symbol of the United States, holds a streamer bearing the state motto, "Our Liberties We Prize and Our Rights We Will Maintain."

The state constitution directs that the governor should have custody of the seal. This was the result of a bitter quarrel between Territorial Governor Robert Lucas and Secretary William Conway. Conway paid for the territorial seal out of his own pocket and expected to be the keeper of it. At first, official papers were issued and signed by the governor and the secretary, who affixed the seal to them. Then the governor took possession of the seal. The secretary demanded its return. He even offered the governor one hundred dollars in gold for return of the seal but to no avail. Conway then protested to the president of the United States and denounced the governor. The bad feeling between the men developed into a bitter feud that ended only with the sudden death of Secretary Conway.

The governor is the custodian of the Great State Seal of Iowa.

Kansas

When Kansas became the thirty-fourth state in 1861, Governor Charles Robinson brought up the matter of a state seal in his first address to the legislature. He said the new constitution required an official seal and appointed a committee of three members from the House and three from the Senate to select a design.

The two groups got together but did not produce a seal very quickly. They deliberated at length on dozens of designs and mottoes. One member suggested a landscape with the motto "We Will." Someone else wanted to change the motto to "We Won't," and no one agreed with anyone else. Meantime state documents went uncertified by a seal. Tired of waiting, the Senate finally sent a message saying they wanted a decision immediately and the committee hastily came to an agreement.

The design, adopted four months after statehood, was historic as well as indicative of the state's industries. The rising sun over the mountain in the East symbolizes the rising importance of

Kansas. The river and steamboat stand for commerce; the plowman and the settler's cabin represent agriculture, while the ox
wagon and herd of buffalo chased by Indians refer to the early
history of the state. At the top is the state motto, *Ad Astra Per
Aspera*—"To the Stars Through Difficulties." Thirty-four stars
below the motto show that Kansas was the thirty-fourth state.

Surrounding the design are the words GREAT SEAL OF THE STATE OF KANSAS and January 29, 1861, date of statehood.

This design was not the one the committee had originally chosen. One of the members, John Ingalls, submitted a sketch consisting of a "blue shield at the base of a cloud, out of which was emerging one silver star to join the constellation in the firmament, comprising the 34 then in the Union." It was simple and unique, satisfied the committee in every respect, and they accepted it. Then some of the "wild heralds of the frontier," who had their own ideas, altered it by mixing a steamboat and plowing, Indians and buffalo, till nothing remained of the original design but the motto.

The governor is custodian of the Great State Seal of Kansas.

✳ ═══ Kentucky ═══ ✳

This state has been called a commonwealth by its lawmakers since 1792. Commonwealth is another name for a state in which the supreme power is held by the people. So Kentucky is commonly referred to as a state and legally as a commonwealth.

Some time after becoming the fifteenth state in 1792, the general assembly appointed a committee to choose a suitable official seal. The committee did a great deal of research and conferring with the governor and finally came up with a design that met with the legislature's approval.

It featured two friends embracing and the motto "United We Stand, Divided We Fall." The men wore tight-fitting knee britches and swallowtail coats and stood very close together with their arms about each other. In the outer circle was COMMON-WEALTH OF KENTUCKY, and at the bottom were branches of goldenrod in bloom, which is the state flower. A later version of this

seal had the men dressed in long, tight-fitting trousers and not in such a warm embrace.

In 1962 the present version of the seal was adopted. Once more the men were regarbed and moved farther apart. Now a frontiersman clasps the shoulder and shakes the hand of the statesman in a swallowtail coat. The frontiersman represents famous Kentucky pioneers such as Daniel Boone; the statesman represents aristocratic intellectuals such as Henry Clay.

The state motto on the seal comes from "The Liberty Song" by John Dickson. It was popular during the Revolutionary War, particularly the stanza:

> Then join in hand
> Brave Americans all
> By uniting we stand
> By Dividing we fall.

The secretary of the commonwealth is custodian of the Great Seal of Kentucky.

 Louisiana

When Louisiana became the eighteenth state in 1812 their first state governor, William C. Claibourne, used a seal of his own choosing. It featured a bird that looked like a "cross between a pelican and an eagle with twelve hungry nestlings." Apparently it was meant to be a pelican. According to a newspaper of 1813 the new state of Louisiana had chosen a pelican for its seal because the bird had the reputation of tearing its breast to feed its young.

The pelican acquired this reputation from a myth that said when there is no food the mother bird tears her breast and feeds her blood to the nestlings. Because of this legend the pelican has become a symbol of charity, mother-love, and self-sacrifice.

During the Civil War, Louisiana seceded and the state divided over the issue. For a while there were two governors, Governor Allen of the Confederate part of the state and Governor Michael Hahn of the Federal section of the state. Both governors used

a pelican seal. Allen's had the pelican's head turned to the left and a nestful of young. Hahn's seal had the bird's head turned to the right and there were four nestlings. Unlike Claibourne's seal, these pelicans looked like pelicans.

After the state reunited and Hahn was governor his version of the seal remained in use until 1870 when the nestlings were reduced to three. According to ornithologists, pelicans have only three young at a time.

During these years the seal had never been officially described and adopted by the legislature. This meant that many variations of the seal were used by different state departments, especially in regard to the number of nestlings. In 1902 an act was passed by the legislature adopting the pelican seal, which is described officially as "a pelican with its head turned toward the left, in a nest three young; the pelican following tradition, in the act of tearing its breast to feed its young." Around the pelican are the words "Union, Justice, Confidence," which is the state motto. The outer circle contains the inscription STATE OF LOUISIANA.

The pelican is not only the official state bird, but it is the symbol of Louisiana and appears on the state flag.

The secretary of state is custodian of the Great State Seal of Louisiana.

 Maine

When Maine became the twenty-third state in 1820, the first state legislature adopted an official seal. As they needed the seal immediately, there was little time to spend on making the sketch. Unfortunately, due to haste, this first design turned over to a die maker was rather crude. Afterwards there were complaints that the moose on the seal resembled a deer with moose horns. The seal used today, cast in 1919, is a more artistic version of the 1820 design. The moose looks like a moose.

The shield in the center of the seal features a Maine mast pine. (These famous pine trees were reserved for use as masts for sailing ships.) The moose represents the abundant wildlife of those days. On the left, the farmer with a scythe stands for agriculture, and the sailor, leaning on his anchor, symbolizes the fishing and shipping industry of Maine. *Dirigo* means "I Guide" or "I Direct" and is the state motto.

Above the motto is the North Star. According to the original

description of the seal, this represented Maine as the most northern state of the Union. Later historians feel that the North Star symbolizes the state and, together with the motto "I Guide" or "I Direct," means that the citizens of Maine look to their state for guidance or direction.

During an election dispute in 1879-80, the Secretary of State

Prince A. Sawyer removed the state seal and important documents from his office. A week later, under threat of legal action, Mr. Sawyer returned the seal. But as a result of this a law was passed making the removal of the state seal from the office of the secretary of state an act punishable by imprisonment of not less than one nor more than five years, and by a fine of not exceeding five thousand dollars. The seal has never been removed again.

The secretary of state is custodian of the Great State Seal of Maine.

✳ ══════ Maryland ══════ ✳

The seal of this state is different from all other state seals because it does not bear the name of the state it represents. "Maryland" does not appear on the seal.

The King of England granted the colony of Maryland to Cecil and Leonard Calvert in the charter of 1632. The colony's official seal, which came from England, was very similar to the seal used today.

When Maryland ratified the Federal Constitution in 1788 to become the seventh of the original thirteen states, it already had a seal. In 1776 the colony had declared its independence from British rule and adopted a state constitution and official seal. It featured the quartered shield, farmer, and fisherman of the colonial seal, but had an eagle perched above the shield and below was the Latin motto *Crescite et Multiplicamini*, meaning "Increase and Multiply." Around this design was the inscription THE GREAT SEAL OF MARYLAND.

For one hundred years this was the state seal until in 1876 Maryland readopted the colonial seal. Though there are two sides to the seal, a reverse and obverse, only the reverse is used officially. The obverse, while considered part of the seal, serves mainly for decoration in public buildings.

The reverse side is probably the most heraldic of all state seals.

The shield in the center is quartered. The first and fourth quarters contain the arms of the Calvert family; the second and third quarters hold the Crossland family arms, which Calvert inherited from his grandmother. The crown, or coronet, above the shield indicates that while Cecil Calvert, the first Lord Baltimore, was only a baron in England, in Maryland he was an earl or count and absolute Lord of Maryland.

Left of the shield is a farmer with a shovel, on the right a fisherman holding a fish. They symbolize the two estates of Lord Baltimore, Maryland and Avalon. Avalon was Lord Baltimore's grant in Newfoundland.

Below the shield, in Italian, is the Calvert family motto, *Fatti Maschii Parole Femine*, meaning "Manly Deeds, Womanly Words." This is one of Maryland's two state mottoes. Behind and surrounding the shield and figures is an ermine-lined cloak, a sign of nobility.

The outer circle contains the second state motto *Scuto Bonae Voluntatis Tuae Coronasti Nos*, which translated from the Latin means "With Favor Wilt Thou Compass Us as with a Shield," taken from Psalm 5, Verse 12. Another translation is "With the Shield of Thy Good-will Thou Hast Covered Us." The date 1632 is that of the first charter.

The secretary of state is custodian of the Great Seal of Maryland.

✳══ Massachusetts ══✳

Like Virginia, Kentucky, and Pennsylvania, Massachusetts is officially a commonwealth but is generally referred to as a state. Commonwealth is but another name for a state in which the supreme power is held by the people.

The first seal of this state dates back to 1629 when King Charles I of England authorized the Massachusetts Bay Colony to use an official seal. That first seal depicted an Indian with an arrow pointing downward in one hand, a bow in the other. From his mouth issued the words, "Come over and help us."

Massachusetts was the sixth state to ratify the Federal Constitution, and in 1780 the state council adopted a design for the seal of the commonwealth submitted by Nathan Cushing. This seal also featured an Indian and was very similar to the colonial seal.

In 1898 the secretary of the commonwealth directed Edmund H. Garrett to redraw the seal design, which was then simplified and made less ornate. This is the seal used today.

In the center of the shield an Indian holds in his left hand an arrow pointing downward to indicate peace, and a bow in his right hand. The five-pointed star represents Massachusetts as a state. Around the shield is the state motto, *Ense Petit Placidam Sub Libertate Quietem*, meaning "By the Sword We Seek Peace, but Peace Only Under Liberty." Above the shield, the arm and sword symbolize the state motto. Surrounding this design, which is also the state coat-of-arms, is inscribed in Latin SIGILLUM REIPUBLICAE MASSACHUSETTENSIS, which translated means "Seal of the Republic of Massachusetts."

The secretary of the commonwealth is the custodian of the Great Seal of Massachusetts.

✳══════ Michigan ══════✳

While still a territory in 1835, Michigan held a constitutional convention and unanimously voted to become a state. The people elected their first governor and adopted the present state seal. This was a highly irregular procedure as only the Federal Government in Washington, D.C., could grant statehood. But for the next two years the territory operated under a state government unrecognized by Washington. Not until 1837 did Michigan officially become the twenty-sixth state. General Lewis Cass designed the seal adopted at that convention in 1835, basing his design on the seal of the Hudson Bay Fur Company.

The United States motto *E Pluribus Unum*—"From Many One"—appears at the top of this seal. Directly below, the American eagle holds three arrows of war in one talon, in the other the olive branch of peace, with thirteen olives for the original states. The eagle, our national bird, symbolizes the authority of the United States to which Michigan "has ever proved herself truly

74

loyal." Within the shield, a rising sun signifies the rising prosperity of the state.

Michigan is on an international border, and the man raises his right hand aloft for peace, but holds a gun in his left to indicate he is ready to defend his state and nation. Above, the word *Tuebor* means "I will defend." Supporting the shield is an elk on the left and a moose on the right, symbols of the state of Michigan.

Below them is the state motto, *Si Quaeris Peninsulam Amoenam Circumspice*—"If You Seek a Pleasant Peninsula, Look About You." Around the border is THE GREAT SEAL OF THE STATE OF MICHIGAN and the date 1835 in Roman numerals. This is the date of the convention that voted to become a state, not their legal date of statehood.

The secretary of state is custodian of the Great State Seal of Michigan.

✳══════ Minnesota ══════✳

When Minnesota was declared a territory in 1849, the legislature could not agree on a design for the official seal. They turned the matter over to Governor Alexander Ramsey and Henry H. Sibley, the territorial delegate to Washington, D.C. These two men decided on a sketch which the legislature adopted as the territorial seal.

This design depicted a white settler and his plow beside the Mississippi River at the falls of St. Anthony. His gun resting against a stump indicated he had set aside his weapon in favor of the peaceful pursuit of agriculture but was ready to defend himself. In the background an Indian on horseback galloped toward the setting sun. At the top was the Latin motto *Quae Sursum Volo Videre*, meaning "I Wish to See What Is Above." Around the design was inscribed THE GREAT SEAL OF MINNESOTA, with the territorial date 1849.

After the seal was cast, several mistakes were discovered. The

Indian galloped toward the sun in the East instead of the West.
This was a grave error, for as white men moved into the territory,
the Indians were forced to flee westward. Also, the engraver had
misspelled the Latin motto. Despite these mistakes, this remained
the territorial seal until 1858 when Minnesota became the thirty-
second state.

Upon attaining statehood there was no official seal yet and the secretary of state wrote Sibley, who was now the governor, "My office being without a seal, I can of course do no official act, unless you make some direction about the matter." Sibley settled the problem by giving the secretary permission to use the territorial seal in the meantime.

A bill approving a new seal design had gone to the legislature for approval, but for some reason it did not become a law. But a law did pass giving the governor authority to have a state seal engraved.

Sibley, who liked the territorial seal he had helped select, had the same design engraved again for the state seal. This time he reversed the galloping Indian so he rode off into the West toward the setting sun, symbolizing the declining days of the red man. He also removed the incorrect Latin motto, replacing it with the French words *L'Étoile du Nord*, meaning "Star of the North." This state motto honors the French explorers who had been the first white settlers in this region.

Inscribed about the design was THE GREAT SEAL OF THE STATE OF MINNESOTA and date of statehood, 1858. The governor used this as the official state seal though it was not adopted by the legislature for three years.

The secretary of state is custodian of the Great State Seal of Minnesota.

✳ ══════ Mississippi ══════ ✳

Judge Daniel Tilton brought Mississippi's territorial seal by boat to Natchez sometime in 1799. It was very similar to the Great Seal of the United States as it featured an American eagle with a shield on its chest. However, on this seal the territory was spelled Missisippi; one "s" had been omitted.

In 1817, upon becoming the twentieth state, the Mississippi Constitution provided for an official state seal much like the territorial one, but the spelling was corrected.

With few minor changes, this is the same state seal in use today. The Federal eagle symbolizes strength and the Union. The olive branch and arrows signify that peace will be offered first and war (represented by the arrows) will only follow if peace has been refused. Surrounding the design are the words THE GREAT SEAL OF THE STATE OF MISSISSIPPI.

Though this state seceded from the Union in 1861 during the

War Between the States, the seal remained unchanged under the Secessionist government.

The governor is in charge of the Great Seal of Mississippi. Because the secretary of state affixes the seal to official documents signed by the governor, the seal is kept in the secretary's office as a matter of convenience, and he is responsible for the safety and security of the seal.

Missouri

By the time Missouri became the twenty-fourth state in 1821, it already had a constitution with provisions for an official seal. But not until the following January did the legislature adopt a seal designed by Robert William Wells, an attorney who later became a federal judge. Apparently Secretary of State W. G. Pettus also had a hand in the design as he selected the bears that are prominent in the seal. According to him the grizzly bear "represented the rugged, positive character of the inhabitants of the new state of Missouri."

In the inner circle of the seal on the right is the coat-of-arms of the United States, an eagle with arrows in its talons. To the left of this is a walking grizzly and above him a crescent new moon indicative of the rise of Missouri's strength and importance. Around these is the motto "United We Stand Divided We Fall." This part of the design signifies that Missouri is independent and yet a part of the Federal government.

At the top of this inner circle, a visored helmet represents strength and power. Directly above the helmet a slightly larger star surrounded by twenty-three smaller stars indicates that Missouri is the twenty-fourth state to join the Union.

Two erect bears support the inner design, and in later years Judge Wells wrote of them that grizzly bears "almost peculiar to the Missouri River and its tributaries, were remarkable for their prodigious size, strength and courage, and show that while we support ourselves by our own internal strength, we also support the general government."

Beneath the design the state motto *Salus Populi Suprema Lex Esto* means "The People Shall Be the Supreme Law." Below, in Roman numerals, is MDCCCXX, 1820, the date of the state constitution. In the outer circle is inscribed THE GREAT SEAL OF THE STATE OF MISSOURI.

The secretary of state is custodian of the Great State Seal of Missouri.

$*$═══Montana═══$*$

For six years after becoming the forty-first state in 1889, Montana continued to use her territorial seal of 1865 because legislators had been unable to agree on a new design. At last the governor demanded action, saying it was "unbecoming the dignity of Montana" to keep using the territorial seal. So, for twenty dollars, they had a jeweler engrave a new die from the old seal merely substituting STATE for TERRITORY. Today's seal closely follows that design.

The seal depicts Montana's economy and future. The plow, shovel, and pick represent agriculture and mining wealth. In the background are the Great Falls of the Missouri River and the mountains from which Montana took its name. *Oro y Plata*, meaning "Gold and Silver," makes this the only state seal with a Spanish motto. Around the design is THE GREAT SEAL OF THE STATE OF MONTANA.

In territorial days the secretary and the governor were joint

custodians of the seal of 1865. The arrangement worked well until 1876 when the secretary, James E. Callaway, decided to charge each time he affixed the seal to an official document to augment his meager salary. He refused to let the governor use the seal as this would bring him no revenue. Governor Benjamin F. Potts had a problem on his hands. The law specified the territorial seal and governor's signature on all official documents. Callaway had the seal and no personal or political persuasion could pry it loose.

Potts ordered another seal. The enraged Callaway aroused the House over the use of two seals and the matter became a partisan controversy. One House member suggested, "Someone," (he did not specify who), "might have a counterfeit territorial seal." The House took no action on this charge but that did not end the matter. Two local newspapers took up the argument, one suggesting that Callaway had the forged seal.

Callaway immediately wrote an open letter to the legislature stating physical possession of the seal rested solely with the secretary, and questioned the legality of bonds, commissions, and pardons certified with the governor's copy of the seal. Again the House refused to become involved, and Potts solved his own problem. When Callaway's reappointment came up, Governor Potts used his political influence in Washington to have another man appointed.

Governor Potts resigned in 1883 and four days later a bill was passed giving custody of the territorial seal to the secretary. Today the secretary of state has custody.

✳══════Nebraska══════✳

This state seal bears not only the year, but the month and day of admission to the Union.

A few weeks after Nebraska became the thirty-seventh state on March 1, 1867, Governor David Butler called a special session of the legislature to start a new state government. Isaac Wiles, representative from Cass County, introduced an act for securing a seal which passed both Houses, and twenty-five dollars "or so much as may be necessary" was appropriated out of the treasury for this purpose.

Mr. Wiles felt very strongly against slavery and suggested two mottoes, both on the subject of freedom. One was "Equal Rights for All," and the other "Equality Before the Law." The second was chosen. Mr. Wiles also described in great detail how the seal should be designed to show the resources of the state: a steamboat ascending the Missouri River for water transportation; train and cars for rail transportation, with the beautiful Rocky Mountains

in the background; a blacksmith, hammer, and anvil representing the mechanics' arts; a settler's cabin with sheaves of wheat and stalks of corn for agriculture. He took this design to a jeweler in Omaha, at that time the capital of Nebraska. For twenty-five dollars the jeweler made the final design and engraved the seal, which was then presented to the first secretary of state, Thomas P. Kennard.

The next year the seal played a vital role in moving the capital from Omaha to Lincoln. This was mainly the work of the governor and Mr. Kennard. They had let out contracts for a new capitol building in Lincoln against the wishes of those who wanted Omaha to remain the capital. The two state officers were threatened with an injunction to prevent them from taking the seal, insignia of the office, to the new location.

Meeting secretly, both men laid their plans and the governor left for his home to prepare a proclamation announcing the moving of the capital to Lincoln. Meanwhile Secretary Kennard went into the capitol on Sunday, took the seal, wrapped it up and hid it under the seat of his buggy. He then drove across the prairie and the Platte River to Lincoln. On Monday morning, December 3, 1868, he arrived at the new capitol building with the state seal and put the impression on Governor Butler's proclamation. This officially made Lincoln the new state capital. Had the state seal not been stolen, Omaha might still be the capital.

The secretary of state is custodian of the Great State Seal of Nebraska.

══════ Nevada ══════

The design for Nevada's Territorial Seal of 1861 was the work of Orien Clemens, secretary of the territory and brother of Samuel Clemens, better known as Mark Twain. This seal featured the mining resources of the state, especially silver, with a background of mountains, water turning the wheel of a quartz mill, a miner leaning on his pick holding an American flag, and the motto *Volens et Potents*—"Willing and Able"—indicating loyalty to the Union and the wealth to sustain it.

Upon becoming the thirty-sixth state in 1864, the secretary of state was authorized to procure a state seal. However, this new seal, though used officially for the next two years, did not become legal until 1866.

Many historians believe that Orien Clemens also designed the state seal because it was so much like the territorial seal in depicting mining and related activities. But the answer to who really designed the seal is lost in the ashes of a huge fire that destroyed

the building and records of the Society of Pacific Coast Pioneers in 1875.

There is a story that Mark Twain offered a design featuring buzzards as he contended "there were more of them in Nevada than quartz mills." He also said the motto *Volens et Potents* applied to buzzards as well as quartz mills. However, Twain was noted for his humor and no one took his suggestion seriously.

The original description of the seal when it was adopted in 1864 was not concise. Succeeding seals varied from the original until 1976 when an act was passed in which there is a complete and legal description of the seal as it is today.

The building at the foot of the mountain on the right is a quartz mill. In the mountain opposite is the tunnel of a silver mine, with a miner running out a carload of ore and a team loaded with ore for the mill. A plow, sickle, and sheaf of wheat symbolize agriculture. The railroad and telegraph line depict Nevada's importance as a corridor between the Midwest and the Coast. Around this design are thirty-five stars, for the number of states in the Union when Nevada joined, and the state motto, "All For Our Country." In the outermost circle is inscribed THE GREAT SEAL OF THE STATE OF NEVADA.

The governor is custodian of the Great State Seal, and the secretary of state has access to it at all times for his official use.

✳ ═══ New Hampshire ═══ ✳

This state's first seal dated from 1775 when it was still a colony. The seal featured a bundle of five arrows, for the five counties of that day, between a fish and a pine tree, which represented the fishing and lumber industries. Around this design were the words SEAL OF THE COLONY OF NEW HAMPSHIRE and a motto "In Unity There Is Strength," both written in Latin. Following the Declaration of Independence, the word COLONY on the seal was changed to STATE.

When New Hampshire created its state constitution in 1784, the legislature adopted a new state seal. This one depicted a ship on the stocks (timbers that hold a ship up during construction), with American banners flying. A rising sun symbolized the rising prosperity of the state. Encircling the design were a laurel wreath and 1784, date when the seal was adopted. Around the outside were the words THE STATE OF NEW HAMPSHIRE, written in Latin.

Over the years, various engravers changed details to suit them-

selves, sometimes adding such items as barrels, a fire, or human figures, to the dismay of historians who did not care for such tampering with the seal.

However, no steps were taken to correct this until 1931 when the governor elected a committee to standardize the design of the seal. The committee worked with the original version of the

1784 seal, making a few changes. English was used instead of Latin for SEAL OF THE STATE OF NEW HAMPSHIRE, and 1784 was changed to 1776, date of the Declaration of Independence and birth of the state. The ship was replaced by the frigate *Raleigh*, flying the first United States flag. While the sun remained the same, a granite boulder, symbol of the state of New Hampshire, appeared on the shore at left.

It was fitting that the state seal should honor the *Raleigh* for the important part she played in United States history during the Revolution. She was New Hampshire's contribution to the war, one of the first ships of the new navy. On August 12, 1777, the *Raleigh* sailed for France escorting the *Alfred*, first flagship of the Continental Navy. The two ships were to bring back sorely needed war material, armaments and military supplies. After three weeks at sea they encountered a convoy of British ships. The smaller, slower *Alfred* waited a few miles away while the *Raleigh*, flying a British flag captured earlier, slipped among the convoy and drew up to the sloop-of-war *Druid*. She fired broadside after broadside into the *Druid* until the vessel was "in wreckage." With the rest of the convoy about to enter the fray, *Raleigh* fled to safety and continued to France. This is the first time the new Stars and Stripes went into action at sea.

The secretary of state is custodian of the Great State Seal of New Hampshire.

✳══New Jersey══✳

This is the third of the original thirteen states to ratify the Federal Constitution. One of the first acts of the new legislature was to order an official seal for New Jersey. The seal was to be of silver, with a design consisting of three plows, figures of Liberty and Ceres, and a horse's head as the crest, or top, of the design. But the engraver, on his own authority, added a sovereign's helmet above the plows and used Roman numerals MDCCLXXVI for 1776, year of the Declaration of Independence. As silver was too soft a metal to bear up under the pressure of stamping documents, a duplicate of this seal was cast in brass for official use.

Over the years as the brass seal became blunted, the impressions were no longer legible, and the Legislature of 1928 authorized a new one made of steel. This one accurately followed the 1776 seal, including the helmet, but replaced the Roman numerals with the Arabic 1776, and added a motto.

The horse's head symbolizes not only agriculture but speed,

strength, and usefulness in war or commerce. The helmet represents sovereignty and the "supremacy of the human mind in all civilized life." Three plows on the heraldic shield signify the importance of agriculture as a state industry. On the left Liberty holds a pole with the cap of freedom on it. On the right, Ceres, Goddess of Earth and Agriculture, holds a Horn of Plenty full of apples, plums, and grapes. At their feet is the state motto, "Liberty and Prosperity," with the date 1776, birth of the state. Surrounding this design are the words THE GREAT SEAL OF THE STATE OF NEW JERSEY.

The secretary of state is custodian of the Great State Seal of New Jersey.

====New Mexico====

This state seal is unusual because the symbol of another country is part of the design.

Long ago when Aztec Indians roamed what is now the Republic of Mexico there was a legend that their God commanded them to search until they found an eagle perched on a cactus, devouring a snake. There, on that spot, the tribe should settle and they would prosper and be happy. The eagle of this legend, the small brown Mexican or harpy eagle, is the symbol of the country of Mexico and part of its flag.

When New Mexico became a territory in 1850, the new government needed an official seal. In designing this seal they retained the eagle from the Mexican flag which had flown for so long over the land, and added a large American eagle to represent bravery, skill, and strength. His protective wing over the smaller eagle indicated the change of sovereignty from Mexico to the United States in 1846. Around this design were the words THE

GREAT SEAL OF THE TERRITORY OF NEW MEXICO and MDCCCL, the territorial date 1850. The state motto below the eagle *Crescit Eundo* means "It Grows as It Goes."

The original seal of 1850 has long since disappeared, but there is an early imprint of it on a loyalty oath signed by Territorial Governor Henry L. Connelly in 1865.

When New Mexico became the forty-seventh state in 1912, a commission was named to select a new design for the state seal. Meantime the territorial seal remained in use with a temporary change in the wording. It now read the GREAT SEAL OF THE STATE OF NEW MEXICO and the date 1912 for statehood. Apparently the commission never found a design it liked better, for no new one was ever presented and the temporary seal has become permanent.

The secretary of state is the custodian of the Great State Seal of New Mexico.

✳════New York════✳

This state was the eleventh of the original thirteen states to ratify the Federal Constitution.

When the New York Provincial Congress of 1777 met, they appointed a committee "to prepare a proper device for a great seal for this State." Since that date there have been minor changes in the seal five times. The seal of today, adopted in 1882, is the fifth and last.

Within the shield, the rising sun on the Hudson River indicates the rising of a new world, and also that this river is an important feature of the state. Ships on the river stand for commerce. A globe of the world with an eagle perched on it forms the crest above the shield. The globe represents America as part of the world. The eagle with outstretched wings, an emblem of the United States, faces West toward the new world and away from the old. Symbolically the eagle proclaims "Westward the course of empire takes its way," meaning the future growth of

the country must be to the West. New York was the first state to use the eagle on her seal and coat-of-arms.

Liberty, at the left of the shield, holds a pole with the cap of freedom on it, and at her feet a discarded crown signifies the end of British rule. On the right, blindfolded Justice holds the scales of mercy in one hand, in the other a sword ready to strike against

Tyranny. Beneath is the state motto *Excelsior*, meaning "Ever Upward." Surrounding the design is the inscription THE GREAT SEAL OF THE STATE OF NEW YORK. This design, without the inscription surrounding it, is also the coat-of-arms and appears on the state flag.

The secretary of state is custodian of the Great Seal of New York.

✳ ═══North Carolina═══ ✳

North Carolina was the twelfth of the original thirteen states to ratify the Federal Constitution.

In December, 1776, their state constitution provided for an official seal "to be kept by the Governor and used by him." For cutting and engraving this first state seal William Tisdale, Esq., received the sum of 150 pounds. It had two sides, an obverse and reverse, depicting Liberty and Ceres, but unfortunately this seal and press were so large and heavy they had to be carried about in a wagon. As the government was still moving around, not yet having settled upon a capital, this worked a great hardship on the governor who complained the "seal had become stationary at the Secretary's office which makes it very inconvenient." He asked that the new seal being made in 1793 be lighter and easier to carry about.

The new seal was smaller and easily handled mainly because Liberty and Ceres were combined on one side of the seal only,

eliminating the second side. But the screws on this press did not work, so the cumbersome old seals had to be used until the new one could be repaired.

Succeeding seals continued to use figures of Liberty and Ceres, but there was no motto until 1893. On this design were the Latin words *Esse Quam Videri*—"To Be Rather Than to Seem"—

and the date May 20, 1775. This is the date of the Mecklenburg Declaration of Independence when Colonel Thomas Polk held a meeting in Charlotte (Mecklenburg County) of twenty-seven prominent men in the county. They renounced allegiance to Britain and signed the Declaration as "a free and independent people."

The final revision of the seal in 1971 shows Liberty, symbol of Freedom, standing on the left with her pole and liberty cap. Seated opposite is Ceres, Goddess of Fruitfulness. Three heads of ripe wheat in her right hand and her left hand resting on a cornucopia represent agriculture. The ship in the background signifies both commerce and the fact that the first colonists came by ship. The state motto appears at the bottom of the design and May 20, 1775, at the top. Around the outside are the words THE GREAT SEAL OF THE STATE OF NORTH CAROLINA.

The governor is custodian of the Great State Seal of North Carolina.

===North Dakota===

Like its sister state South Dakota, the question of which is the thirty-ninth or fortieth state cannot be resolved. President Benjamin Harrison deliberately shuffled the documents granting statehood to both Dakotas in 1889 before and after signing. In this way he did not give preference to either state.

When both states were the Territory of Dakota, the Second Legislative Assembly of 1892-93 adopted a territorial seal and motto suggested by Dr. Joseph Ward of Yankton. This seal featured a tree in an open field, its trunk bound with a bundle of rods. There was also an Indian on horseback chasing a buffalo toward the setting sun in the West. In the foreground were farm implements and a bow crossed with three arrows. Above the tree were thirteen stars for the original states, and over the stars the motto "Liberty and Union, One and Inseparable, Now and Forever." This quotation from Daniel Webster was incorrect.

When North Dakota attained statehood it elected to keep the

territorial seal with a few revisions. The motto was changed to quote Webster accurately. Some of the farm implements were omitted and forty-two stars replaced the original thirteen. By the time North Dakota held its first state convention and adopted the new seal, Washington and Montana had joined the Union, making forty-two states at that time.

Still on the seal was the tree in an open field on level land suggesting the North Dakota prairie. Bundles of wheat surrounding the tree and a plow represented agriculture. An anvil and sledge hammer in the foreground symbolized the future industry of the state. The bow and arrows laid to one side and the Indian and buffalo disappearing toward the West indicated that the days of the Indian and buffalo were drawing to a close.

The corrected state motto, "Liberty and Union, Now and Forever, One and Inseparable," shows the state's loyalty to the Union.

In the outer circle is inscribed GREAT SEAL STATE OF NORTH DAKOTA and the date October 1st, 1889, the day North Dakota signed the state constitution.

The secretary of state is custodian of the Great Seal of North Dakota.

 Ohio

Ohio adopted a state constitution one year before it became the seventeenth state in 1803. This constitution provided for an official seal but until it could be procured, Secretary of State William Creighton used his private seal for official documents.

In the spring of 1803, Secretary Creighton along with the governor and others met at a private home to discuss state affairs. The discussion lasted all night. As the weary officials were leaving, they stood for a while on the lawn of the house watching the sun rise slowly from behind a mountain. Filled with admiration for the beauty of the scene, Secretary Creighton exclaimed, "The rising sun of the new state." This became the basis for the Great State Seal of Ohio which the legislature adopted. That seal was the same as today's with one minor change. On the seal of 1803, the sun rose over a single mountain; today's version shows the sun rising over a range of the Alleghenies.

The rising sun which so caught the secretary's imagination

signified that Ohio was the first state west of the Alleghenies. But also, in heraldry the rising sun with rays means a state or empire. On the right a sheaf of wheat standing in the field symbolized the importance of agriculture to this state. On the left a bundle of seventeen arrows indicated that with Ohio there were now seventeen states in the Union. This design, without an inscription around it, is also the state coat-of-arms.

In a double circle surrounding the design are the words THE GREAT SEAL OF THE STATE OF OHIO. Only the governor uses this seal. The other officials each have their own seal consisting of the coat-of-arms surrounded by the name of their office. Therefore, the secretary of state's seal reads THE SEAL OF THE SECRETARY OF STATE OF OHIO.

✳══════ Oklahoma ══════✳

On the morning of November 16, 1907, President Theodore Roosevelt, using an eagle quill pen, signed his name with a flourish to the proclamation making Oklahoma the forty-sixth state.

The seal adopted by the new state is the same as the one used today. It features a five-pointed star in the center of which is the territorial seal and the state motto, *Labor Omnia Vincit*, meaning "Labor Conquers All Things." The upper point of the star contains the symbol of the Chickasaw Nation, an Indian warrior with a bow and shield. The upper left point holds the Cherokee Nation symbol, a seven-pointed star with a wreath of oak leaves. In the lower left point is the symbol of the Creek Nation, a sheaf of wheat and a plow. The lower right point contains the symbol of the Seminole Nation, a village with houses and factory beside a lake on which an Indian paddles a canoe. The upper right point holds the Choctaw Nation symbol, a tomahawk, bow, and three crossed arrows. Around the star, in five clusters of nine each, are

forty-five stars for the number of states in the Union to which the forty-sixth is now added. Surrounding this design is inscribed GREAT SEAL OF THE STATE OF OKLAHOMA and 1907, date of statehood.

The territorial seal in the middle of the star depicts a figure of Columbia representing Justice and Statehood. Beneath the scales of Justice, an American pioneer farmer and an American Indian shake hands. This symbolizes equal justice for the white and red races of Oklahoma. Below them is a Horn of Plenty and olive branch of peace. Behind is the scene of progress and civilization— a farmer plowing, homes, a train, grain mills, factories, churches, and schools. This scene is symbolic of the peaceful conquest by the white man.

When Oklahoma attained statehood the constitutional convention selected a committee to design a state seal. Gabe E. Parker, a Choctaw Indian and member of the committee, wrote to a friend for suggestions. His friend offered Parker a seal design for the proposed state of Sequoyah which had never materialized. This design consisted of a five-pointed star containing the symbols of the five Indian nations.

This idea was combined with the territorial seal and Japp E. Peddicord, a newspaper reporter, made the first draft. The original pencil sketch is now on exhibit at the Museum of the Oklahoma Historical Society in Oklahoma City.

The secretary of state is custodian of the Great State Seal of Oklahoma.

Oregon

Anticipating statehood, Oregon's Constitutional Convention of 1857 adopted a state seal two years before becoming the thirty-third state in 1859.

Every item in this seal designed by Harvey Gordon has an historical meaning. Thirty-three stars surrounding the shield indicate that Oregon was the thirty-third state. Above the shield a Federal eagle with spread wings represents the union of states. The eagle holds an olive branch and three arrows to signify peace through strength.

A departing British man-of-war under full sail symbolizes the withdrawing of British influence, while the arriving American merchant ship indicates the rise of American power. The sun sinking in the Pacific Ocean stands for the West; an elk at the foot of the mountain represents the abundant game which attracted settlers to this region.

An ox-drawn covered wagon is a reminder that Oregon was

settled by pioneers who made the long and dangerous journey in
these wagons. Standing timber nearby represents the lumber industry which is so important to Oregon. The state motto, "The
Union," recalls that Oregon remained loyal to the Union when
the Civil War threatened to split the country.

Agriculture and mining are indicated by the plow and miner's pickax. The sheaf of wheat is an historical reminder that thousands of early settlers survived the first rigorous Oregon Territory winter on a diet of boiled wheat. Surrounding all these are STATE OF OREGON and 1859, date of statehood.

The secretary of state is custodian of the Great Seal of Oregon.

✳ ═══ Pennsylvania ═══ ✳

Pennsylvania, second of the thirteen original states to ratify the Federal Constitution, is legally a commonwealth but generally referred to as a state. Commonwealth is an English term meaning "a state in which the supreme power is held by the people." Unlike the other commonwealths, Virginia, Kentucky, and Massachusetts, Pennsylvania uses the word STATE on her seal.

King Charles II of England in 1681 granted what is now Pennsylvania to William Penn. For the official seal of the colony, Penn used his family arms surrounded with the inscription WILLIAM PENN PROPRIETOR & GOVERNOR OF PENSILVANIA. Some time later the spelling was changed to Pennsylvania.

With Independence in 1776, the commonwealth approved a design for a new seal but did not legally adopt it until 1791. This seal was the basis of today's design, having a ship, plow, and three sheaves of wheat. The seal was the combination of the crests of the seals of three counties of Pennsylvania. The crest on the seal

of Chester County was a plow; the crest on the seal of Philadelphia County was a ship under full sail. The sheaves of wheat were from the seal of Sussex County, which later became a part of Delaware. Around the design were the words SEAL OF THE STATE OF PENNSYLVANIA.

When this seal wore out in 1809 some changes were made in

the new one. A shield with an eagle crest was added and the ship, plow, and wheat were placed in the shield. On the left appeared a stalk of Indian corn, symbolic of the Indians who were friendly to the first settlers; on the right, an olive branch of peace. Strangely, the inscription around this seal read from right to left instead of the usual left to right. In 1858 this was corrected and SEAL OF THE STATE OF PENNSYLVANIA went from left to right as in all other seals.

The present seal, adopted in 1893, had only a few minor changes. A wreath of flowers above the shield was eliminated, and the ship and plow faced right to left instead of left to right as formerly.

The secretary of the commonwealth is custodian of the Great Seal of Pennsylvania.

✳══ Rhode Island ══✳

and Providence Plantations

This is the smallest state in the Union, but its seal bears the longest official name and the shortest motto of any other state seal.

The colony of Rhode Island denounced allegiance to the British King in May, 1776, even before the Declaration of Independence, but did not ratify the Federal Constitution until 1790 making it the last of the original thirteen colonies to do so.

Early settlements of the colony were called plantations, and in 1647 the four largest, Providence, Warwick, Portsmouth, and Newport, were incorporated under the name of Providence Plantations. Rhode Island, part of the colony, was a large island in the bay.

The official seal of this colony was very simple, consisting only of a plain anchor and no motto. Anchors were often used as the device on seals in those days, but possibly being surrounded by the sea may have had a bearing on the choice of an anchor.

A new charter in 1663 changed the name of the colony to Rhode Island and Providence Plantations. This made it necessary to have a new seal. The new one, engraved in 1664, featured a foul anchor (an anchor with a cable twisted about the shank), and the word "Hope" appeared for the first time. Historians believe "Hope" was selected from the Bible phrase, "Hope we have as an anchor of the soul." Since the colony was founded by religious leaders, that could very well have influenced their choice of motto.

Several seals were made after the 1664 design, all bearing the foul anchor device. Not until 1892 was another seal engraved that reverted to the original plain anchor, and this is the design in use today. The state motto, "Hope," appears above the anchor and surrounding them are the words SEAL OF THE STATE OF RHODE ISLAND AND PROVIDENCE PLANTATIONS, with the date 1636. This is the date Roger Williams founded the settlement of Providence. He is also considered the founder of the colony of Rhode Island.

The secretary of state is custodian of the Great Seal of Rhode Island and Providence Plantations.

✳══ South Carolina ══✳

South Carolina is one of the two states that uses both sides of their seal. Virginia is the other one. Many state seals do have two sides, a "reverse" and "obverse," as does the United States Great Seal. But usually only the reverse is used officially. In the case of South Carolina, one side is called the "arms," and the other "reverse." Both are combined into one large seal.

The eighth state to ratify the Federal Constitution, South Carolina immediately required an official state seal. William H. Drayton, member of the council, prepared the arms side, while Arthur Middleton designed the reverse. Both men based their work on a successful battle against the British on June 28, 1776, at Sullivan's Island.

The left, or arms, side of the seal shows a palmetto tree. This symbolizes Sullivan Island's fort which was built of palmetto logs. At the base of the tree lies a torn-up oak with its branches chopped

off to represent the defeated British Fleet which was constructed
of oak.

Hanging from the palmetto are two shields; one bears the date
March 26, the other July 4. The first date is that of the signing
of the Constitution of South Carolina; the second is for the Declaration of Independence. Twelve spears tied to the tree represent

the first twelve states in the Union, and the ribbon binding them reads *Quis Separabit*—"Who Shall Separate." Under the fallen oak are the words *Meliorem Lapsa Locavit*—"Having Fallen It Has Set Up Better." Below is 1776, date of our Independence. Encircling the arms side of the seal is SOUTH CAROLINA and *Animis Opibusque Parati*—"Prepared in Mind and Resource." This is one of the state's two mottoes.

On the right, or reverse side, a woman walks along the seashore over swords and daggers. She represents Hope overcoming dangers which the rising sun is about to disclose. A laurel branch in her hand symbolizes the victory at Sullivan's Island, and she looks toward the bright sun indicating the battle was fought on a fine day. The sun also "bespeaks good fortune." Beneath her is the word *Spes*—"Hope," and above her in the outer circle is the state's second motto *Dum Spiro Spero*—"While I Breathe I Hope."

The secretary of state is custodian of the Great Seal of South Carolina, which is much larger than most state seals, being four inches in diameter.

✳ ══ South Dakota ══ ✳

South Dakota is either the thirty-ninth or fortieth state. President Harrison shuffled the two proclamations granting statehood to both Dakotas in 1889 before and after signing them. In this way he did not give preference to either state.

Both states had comprised the Territory of Dakota and their Legislative Assembly of 1862-63 adopted a territorial seal. This design pictured the troublesome beginnings of the Dakota territory. There was an Indian hunting a buffalo, farm implements, a bow with three crossed arrows, and a tree bound with a bundle of rods. Above the tree were thirteen stars for the original states and over the stars the motto "Liberty and Union, One and Inseparable, Now and Forever."

Statehood required a new seal for each state and the legislative session of 1889 appointed a committee to find an appropriate seal design for South Dakota. Mr. H. H. Blair, a cabinetmaker and druggist by trade but very artistic, worked with Dr. Joseph Ward,

one of the committee members on this. The doctor could not draw at all but had a design in mind which he described in detail to Mr. Blair. Mr. Blair worked all night making a pencil sketch. The legislature adopted this design and it is the one used today.

The seal features the industries of the state such as the smelting furnace for mining and the steamboat on the river for transportation and commerce. Cattle in the background represent grazing and dairying, while the farmer plowing his field indicates South Dakota is an agricultural state. At the top of the design is the state motto, "Under God the People Rule," and the outer circle contains STATE OF SOUTH DAKOTA—GREAT SEAL and 1889, date of statehood.

In 1961 Richard Cropp of Mitchell, South Dakota, made a colored version of the seal. An act providing for an official colored Great Seal of the State adopted Mr. Cropp's work. This colored seal is kept by the secretary of state in a container sealed against sunlight and is the basis for all color reproductions of the state seal.

The secretary of state is custodian of the Great Seal of South Dakota.

✳ ══════ Tennessee ══════ ✳

Before Tennessee became a state it was part of the Territory South of the Ohio River. Unlike most territories they had no territorial seal. Promptly upon becoming the sixteenth state in 1796, the new state constitution provided for an official seal but no action was taken on this for five years. Meanwhile, the governor used his personal seal on documents. At last, in 1801, a committee was appointed "to prepare a device and motto," and the design adopted then is almost the same as today's seal.

That seal was 2½ inches in diameter and across the top were the Roman numerals XVI, indicating that Tennessee was the sixteenth state. The plow, sheaf of wheat, and cotton plant with the word "Agriculture" represented the importance of farming to the state. The lower part of the circle contained a boat and a boatman with the word "Commerce," which attested to the importance of river traffic. Around this design were the words

THE GREAT SEAL OF THE STATE OF TENNESSEE and the date Feb. 6, 1796, date of statehood.

William and Matthew Atkinson of Jonesboro made the first seal and press and delivered them to Governor Archibald Roane in April, 1802. A few days later the governor used the new seal for the first time on an official warrant of payment for one hundred dollars to the Atkinsons.

As dies wore out and were replaced, variations appeared in the seal. During 1866 and 1867 Governor William Brownlow used two seals but finally settled on the one used today. Under his administration slight changes were made. Feb. 6 was omitted and only the year 1796 retained. A more up-to-date riverboat replaced the man in the rowboat.

The governor of Tennessee is custodian of the Great Seal of Tennessee.

✳ ══════ Texas ══════ ✳

This state has probably the most colorful history in the Union. Six flags have flown over Texas. It was an independent republic with its own navy and recognized by the United States before becoming a state. Yet it has one of the least ornate seals, bearing neither date nor motto.

The 1836 first congress of the Republic of Texas approved a national seal consisting of a single star with the words REPUBLIC OF TEXAS surrounding it. Somehow this seal was lost. Years later it turned up on a farm just before the Civil War. The farmer, not realizing what it was, used it as a tool for driving tacks into boots and for cracking pecans. He later gave it to a lady who collected historic things, and in 1936 the long-lost original national seal of the republic won first prize as the most interesting historical exhibit at the Texas Centennial.

Three years after the adoption of the 1836 seal, it was replaced by another seal in 1839. This design stipulated "a white

star of five points on an azure ground encircled by an olive branch and a live oak branch and the words Republic of Texas surrounding them." The star is the symbol of Texas; the olive branch represents peace; and the live oak, native to Texas, stands for strength and fertility. Peter Krag, an artist, drew the design for which he received eight dollars. For another ten dollars he drew the Republican national flag, the lone star banner, which still flies over Texas.

Upon becoming the twenty-eighth state in 1845, the wording on the seal was changed to THE STATE OF TEXAS. At that time only the governor kept the seal and it was used solely by him. Not until 1876 did custody of the seal pass from the governor to the secretary of state.

In 1961 the Texas adjutant general wanted to use the state seal in color on the nose of National Guard airplanes. But he found there was no one standard for color reproductions of the seal. Each artist had his own version of an azure background and used any shade of blue he liked. The leaves of the branches were never the same green. In fact, in some reproductions, a Spanish oak was substituted for the original live oak branch. The adjutant general and a group of Texans interested in historical accuracy for their state seal researched it, going back to the original sketch by Peter Krag and the 1839 bill which had stated the colors. When they had the information, an artist painted a watercolor of the seal which is accurate in every detail and exactly as the Texas Constitution intended it to be. This painting is the official stand-ard for all color reproductions of the Great State Seal of Texas.

Utah

Immediately upon becoming the forty-fifth state in 1896, Utah adopted their present state seal. Harry Edwards, member of the National Society of Artists, drew the design. It was then turned over to an engraver, who for sixty-five dollars made the seal.

The beehive in the center of the shield is a symbol in Utah history and appeared on their territorial seal of 1851. Now it is the official emblem of Utah. The sego lilies growing on both sides of the beehive also have historical significance. The root, or bulb, of this plant saved Utah pioneers from starvation in 1848 when they ran out of food and their crops had not matured.

The date 1847 represents the year the first permanent white settlers, the Mormons, came to Utah. "Industry" as the state motto only became official in 1959 when the state legislature adopted it. However, it had been the unofficial motto for many years and appeared on the 1896 seal.

The American eagle with spread wings, the two American

flags, and the six arrows piercing the upper part of the shield symbolize patriotism and power. Surrounding the design are the words THE GREAT SEAL OF THE STATE OF UTAH and the date of statehood, 1896.

The Utah Historical Society in Salt Lake City has the original design of the state seal of 1896, a watercolor signed by Harry Edwards. The secretary of state is custodian of the Great State Seal of Utah.

✳ ══════ Vermont ══════ ✳

When Vermont joined the Union in 1781 and became the four-teenth state, it already had an official seal. Fourteen years before, in 1777, Vermont had declared its independence and adopted a constitution which provided for a seal. This seal was designed by Ira Allen, Revolutionary War hero and brother of Ethan Allen. For two days Ira worked on the sketch which the general assembly adopted in 1779. A local silversmith engraved the die, probably out of silver as it wore out in 1821 and was replaced by a slightly different seal. As succeeding dies wore out, Vermont had five different seals.

When the fifth seal, cast in 1898, had to be replaced the Vermont Historical Society requested the General Assembly of 1937 to "restore the original symbolic design of 1779" as the state seal. The assembly approved the bill and it became a law.

Tiffany & Co. was commissioned to do the work. As the original die had long been lost, old impressions of the first seal had

to be photographed, enlarged, and sketched from the pictures. The third sketch was finally approved, traced on steel, and cut by hand. This exact replica of the 1779 design is the official seal today.

Too many years have passed to know exactly what Ira Allen intended his design to mean. Historians believe the row of trees across the middle depicts the Green Mountains. The four sheaves of wheat either stand for agriculture or, as some researchers think, represent the four counties of 1777. The cow stands for dairying, while the object opposite the cow could be a spearhead symbolizing the "danger to Vermont at that time from the State of New York." The border is intended to represent arrowheads. Outstanding on this seal is the pine tree with fourteen branches. It is likely that Ira Allen selected the pine tree as a symbol of the United States, with a branch for each of the fourteen states. He depicts the tree with no one dominant branch to mean "the Union should have no one dominant state; that it was a living growing organism, capable of adding branch after branch as it went higher and grew stronger." Obviously this represents the Union adding state after state, becoming larger and greater in strength.

The state motto, "Freedom & Unity," has two interpretations. It can mean the people of Vermont wished to be free and united, or that individual states should be free but united.

The secretary of state is custodian of the Great State Seal of Vermont.

✳ ══════ Virginia ══════ ✳

Virginia, tenth of the original thirteen states to ratify the Federal Constitution, is officially a commonwealth but generally referred to as a state. It is one of the two states which uses two sides of the Great Seal, the obverse and reverse. Impressions of the two seals are attached to state documents. There is also a Lesser Seal of the commonwealth, a smaller version of the obverse seal.

A committee to select a state seal was headed by Chairman George Mason and included George Wythe, a classical scholar. Wythe is credited with doing most of the work, taking his theme from ancient Roman mythology. This design, which was adopted by the Virginia Convention of 1776, was never properly cast and over the years as new dies were made there were variations in the design.

To correct this, a committee was named in 1930 to prepare an accurate and faithful description of the Great Seal of this commonwealth as it was intended by Mason, Wythe, and their associ-

OBVERSE

REVERSE

ates. This committee established the official seal of today, which has the same theme as the 1776 design. The legislature authorized the new seals to be made in accordance with the committee's findings.

The obverse of the seal shows the Roman Goddess Virtus, representing the genius of the commonwealth. Dressed as an Amazon, sheathed sword in one hand, in the other she holds a grounded spear to indicate peace. One foot is on the form of Tyranny, pictured with a broken chain in his left hand, a scourge in his right, and a fallen crown nearby. This symbolizes the struggle with Britain that ended in victory. The state motto below, *Sic Semper Tyrannis*, means "Thus Always to Tyrants."

On the reverse of the seal is the word *Perseverando*, which means "By Persevering," and beneath this are the three Roman goddesses. The center is Libertas (Liberty) with staff and liberty cap; Aeternitis (Eternity) on the left holds a globe and a phoenix; Ceres (Fruitfulness), symbolizing agriculture, is on the right with a cornucopia in one hand and an ear of wheat in the other. Both seals are bordered with a wreath of Virginia creeper.

These two seals are affixed to documents signed by the governor which are to go out of the state or to foreign countries. The lesser seal is used on appointments of state officials, notaries, and documents that remain within the state.

The secretary of the commonwealth is custodian of the Great and Lesser Seals of Virginia.

✳ ═══ Washington ═══ ✳

It is appropriate that the Great Seal of this state should feature the head of George Washington. However, this was not so on their territorial seal.

That seal was designed by Lieutenant J. K. Duntan, member of the governor's surveying party. The lieutenant foresaw great things for the territory and his design pictured a city with spires and domes symbolizing a bright future. The past was represented by a forest and a settler's log cabin. In the foreground the Goddess of Hope pointed upward to an Indian word *Al-ki*, meaning "By and By." Below the goddess was the territorial date 1853.

Thirty-six years later, when Washington became the forty-second state in 1889, a committee was appointed to select a state seal. They chose a very ornate design, took it to the Talcott Brothers, jewelers in Olympia, and asked them to engrave the die. The Talcotts pointed out that they could not successfully get in Mount Rainier, port of Tacoma, and wheatfields on the die.

Instead, George Talcott put a bottle of ink on a piece of paper and drew around it. He then put a silver dollar in the circle and traced around that. Within the two circles he lettered THE SEAL OF THE STATE OF WASHINGTON, 1889. Laying a postage stamp in the middle, he said, "That represents the bust of Washington." The legislature immediately adopted this simple, dignified design.

When the Talcotts made the final drawing they copied the picture of George Washington from an advertisement for Dr. Jayne's Cough and Cold Cure that was popular at the time. There was no place in this design for the Indian word *Al-ki*, but it is still the state motto.

Over the years, as new seals were made, the picture of George Washington went through many changes. Sometimes he faced one way, sometimes another. He was shown as a general and other times as a statesman. In 1966 these discrepancies came to the attention of the governor. He instructed the State Art Commission to select a standard version of the Talcott seal of 1889. Under the direction of the secretary of state, Richard Nelms, a designer, reproduced a famous Gilbert Stuart portrait of Washington in engraver's technique. This version of the seal was made into a law by the 1967 legislature.

The secretary of state is custodian of the Great State Seal of Washington.

✻══════West Virginia══════✻

The first legislature convened on June 20, 1863, the day West Virginia became the thirty-fifth state. Being without a seal or coat-of-arms, a resolution was adopted the second day of the sessions appointing a committee to select a seal and coat-of-arms for the new state. Until an official seal could be obtained, the governor was authorized to use his private seal for state documents.

The Committee on Seals approached Mr. J. H. Diss De Bar of Doddridge County and requested him to create the designs. This gentleman, a landholder in the county and active in local politics, was also known as an artist of considerable ability. A few months later the House and Senate adopted his designs for the obverse and the reverse sides of a state seal and the coat-of-arms. Only the obverse is used as the official state seal.

In the center of the design is a rock with the date of statehood, June 20, 1863, as if "graven with a pen of iron in the rock for-

ever." Climbing over the rock is ivy, emblem of stability. On the left a farmer, with the plow, a sheaf of ripe wheat at his feet, and a corn stalk "in silk" in one hand, represents agriculture. His other hand holds an ax to indicate that the territory, though partly cultivated, was still in the process of being cleared of the forests.

On the right a miner, a pickax on his shoulder with barrels of petroleum and lumps of coal at his feet, anvil and sledge hammer at his side, represents the mineral resources of the state. In front of the rock lie two hunter's rifles, crossed, and surmounted by a Phrygian cap. This cap is a symbol of heroism and victory, signifying "our freedom and liberty were won and will be maintained by the force of arms." Surrounding the design are the words STATE OF WEST VIRGINIA and the state motto, *Montani Semper Liberi*, meaning "Mountaineers Always Free." A smaller version of this seal is called the Lesser Seal and used for less important state papers.

The secretary of state is custodian of the Great State Seal and the Lesser State Seal of West Virginia.

Wisconsin

The Wisconsin Territory, created in 1836, adopted a seal designed by the Honorable John S. Horner, first secretary of the territory. His design featured "an arm holding a pick and an irregular pile of pig lead" (smelted ingots).

When Wisconsin became the thirtieth state in 1848, the new state seal was practically a reproduction of the territorial seal. However, Governor Nelson Dewey did not like the seal and ordered a new design from the chancellor of the University of Wisconsin. He took this design to New York to have it engraved and while there met a friend and showed it to him. His friend did not like the design at all and thought between them they could do much better. The two men sat down together on the steps of one of the banks in Wall Street and worked out the present version of the seal.

By 1881 this seal wore out from use and a new one had to be engraved. Henry Mitchell, a Boston engraver, made some minor

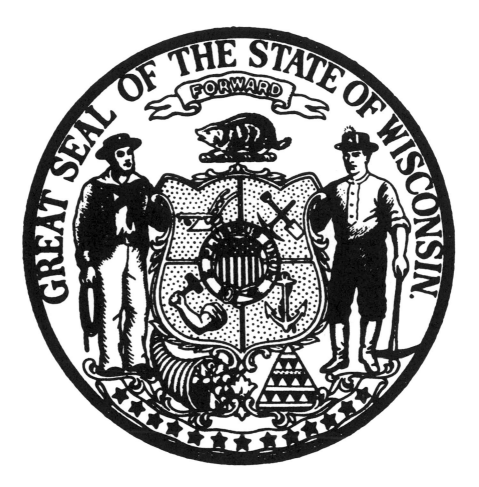

artistic changes in the design which remain in the seal today.

Around the outer edge are the words GREAT SEAL OF THE STATE
OF WISCONSIN, and at the lower edge are thirteen stars for the
original states. The rest of the seal is Wisconsin's coat-of-arms.
A shield divided into fourths bears a plow for agriculture, an arm
holding a hammer for manufacturing, a crossed shovel and pickax

for mining, and an anchor for navigation. Within the shield is a smaller one with thirteen stripes as shown on the Great Seal of the United States. Around this small shield is a double circle on which appears the motto of the nation, *E Pluribus Unum*—"One Out of Many." These two shields symbolize the loyalty of Wisconsin to the Union.

The large shield rests on a pyramid of lead ingots, indicating mineral wealth, and a cornucopia (Horn of Plenty), representing the resources and prosperity of the state. The sailor on the left stands for labor on water; the miner on the right stands for labor on land. Above the shield is the state symbol, the badger, and over him is the state motto, "Forward."

The secretary of state is custodian of the Great State Seal of Wisconsin.

✳ ══ Wyoming ══ ✳

Two dates appear on the Great Seal of this state—1869 commemorating the territorial government, and 1890 the year of statehood.

The number 44 on the shield shows that Wyoming was the forty-forth state admitted into the Union. The woman holding a banner with the state motto, "Equal Rights," indicates that this state has always granted equal civil and political rights to women. It was the first state to do so. As shown by their clothes and equipment, the two men represent livestock and mining. The Light of Knowledge burns on each of the two pillars and the scrolls encircling these pillars bear the words "Oil, Mines, Livestock, Grain," four of Wyoming's major industries.

In 1890 when Wyoming became a state, lawmakers decided to replace the territorial seal with the state seal. Three men were appointed to select the new seal and committee member H. E. Buechner submitted the design that was chosen. However, Sena-

tor Fennimore Chatterton, chairman of the committee, had a design exactly like Buechner's, except the female figure on Chatterton's was nude.

The House passed an act accepting Buechner's design and attached it to the documents accompanying the act. These were then sent to Acting Governor Amos Barber for his signature.

But the committee made a mistake in sending Chatterton to deliver the documents. When the governor received the papers, Chatterton had substituted his own drawing with the nude figure for Buechner's design. The governor failed to notice the switch, signed the act, and the deception passed unnoticed for several months.

When Buechner found out what had happened, he was furious and took the story to the editor of the local newspaper. On March 5, 1891, the *Cheyenne Daily Leader* published their version of the false design. "The figure is supposably that of a Greek slave. This interesting female stands upon what is intended to represent a platform, it is believed, but in reality resembles a large shallow pan or beer vat in which the lady might, without much stretch of imagination, be credited with soaking her corns. Her face is represented in profile and the exuberance of her nose, which is relatively of the same size as one of her feet, is the joy and delight of every beholder."

Because the legislative act adopted Buechner's design and Chatterton's was substituted, the law was declared unconstitutional. The territorial seal went back into use until 1893 when the second legislature passed a law adopting Buechner's design. This was slightly revised in 1921.

The secretary of state is custodian of the Great Seal of Wyoming.

Annemarie Berg, born in Brussels, Belgium, came to the United States when she was ten years old, and her parents immediately became citizens of this country.

As a youngster she excelled in sports, winning state and regional diving championships. She combined a love of sports with love of reading, especially history. When she began writing it was natural for her to write about the history of sports and American history. Her articles have appeared in *Sports Illustrated, True West, Lady Golfer, California Highway Patrolman, Nevada State Magazine, Spinning Wheel, Highlights for Children*, and Sunday supplements.

She is married and lives in Sunnyvale, California.

DATE DUE

DEMCO NO. 38-298